북창삼우

김종회 제5디카시집

도서출판 상상인

북창삼우

작가의 말

다섯 번째 디카시집을 펴낸다. 제4시집 『영감과 섬광』 이후 1년 6개월 만이다. 표제를 '북창삼우'라 한 것은 예로부터 북향 선비의 방에 있던 세 벗, 곧 시와 술과 거문고의 의미를 소환하기 위해서다. 내게 있어 시는 사유思惟를, 취흥은 문향文香을, 그리고 음률은 삶의 리듬을 뜻한다. 이렇게 디카시는 내 일상의 예술이요 예술의 일상이 되었다.

1부 '생활의 새 발견'은 내 삶터 인근의 풍광을 담았다. 2부 '소공녀의 축일'은 사랑하는 손녀와 함께한 시편들이다. 3부 '풍경 속의 잔상'은 국내외 여행지에서의 소회를 포착한 결과다. 4부 '사람과 그 생각'은 특별한 사람 또는 상황의 풍정風情을 한데 모았다. 영문 번역을 해주신 이승희 교수님과 소담스러운 시집으로 묶어주신 도서출판 상상인의 진혜진 대표님께 깊이 감사드린다.

2025년 11월 늦가을
소나기마을 촌장실에서 김종회

A Foreword

This is my fifth Dica-poems collection. It's been a year and six months since my fourth collection, "Inspiration and Flash," came out. I titled this collection "Bukchang Samwoo(北窓三友)" literally translated as North Window Three Friends. The origin of the phrase "Bukchang Samwoo" lies in the fact that since ancient times, a scholar's room facing north had three friends: poetry, wine, and the geomungo, Korean zither. I evoked this meaning in the title of my collection. To me, poetry has three meanings. First, it invites contemplation. Second, the exhilaration of poetry represents the fragrance of literature. And third, the rhythm of poetry signifies the rhythm of life. In this way, Dica-poem has become the art of my daily life, and at the same time, it has become the daily life of my art.

In Part 1, "Life's New Discovery," I captured the scenery near my home. Part 2, "The Little Princess's Festival Days," contains poems from my time with my beloved granddaughter. The poems in Part 3, "The Unforgettable Images of Scenery," are the result of reflections borne during domestic and international travels. The poems in Part 4, "People and The Thoughts," are a collection of poems that accompany the atmosphere of special people or situations. I am deeply grateful to Professor Lee Sung-hee for the English translation, and to Jin Hye-jin, CEO of Sangsangin Publishing, for compiling this charming collection.

November, 2025
Jonghoi Kim, in the Chief's Office of Sonagi Village

차례

1부

생활의 새 발견
Life's New Discovery

전원주택의 벚꽃 Cherry blossoms of a Country House	13
눈꽃 1 Snow Flowers 1	15
눈꽃 2 Snow Flowers 2	17
눈꽃 미소 Snow Flowers' Smile	19
눈 마당 The Snowy Yard	20
눈을 진 노송 An Old Tree with Snow on Its Back	23
설경 문학관 The Snowy Scenery Literary Museum	25
애틋한 사랑 마타리꽃 The Earnest Love Yellow Patrinia	27
황금 깃발 Golden Flag	29
북창삼우 Bukchang Samwoo	31
발자국 Footprints	33
양수리 찬가 Praise for Yangsuri Village	35
적송 Red Pine	37
휴식 Rest	38
모색 Sunsetting Evening	40

2부

소공녀의 축일
A Little Princess's Festival Days

곰돌이 Teddy Bear	45
궁리 Much Thinking	47
균형 A Balance	48
기다리는 마음 Waiting Mind	51
만보기 A Ten-thousand Pace Counter	53
맑음 Clearness	55
모닝 빵순이 Morning Bread Girl	57
소공녀 A Little Princess	59
아침 운동 Morning Exercise	61
어린 예술가 A Child Artist	63
위나비니 천국 Weeny Beeny Heaven	64
작은 공주님 Dear Little Princess	67
전문가 An Expert	68
조손 합심 Grandmother and Granddaughter's Cooperation	71
청명 Bright Clearness	73

3부

풍경 속의 잔상
Unforgettable Images of Scenery

양양 휴휴암 앞바다 The Sea off Hyu-hyu Rock Yangyang	77
해변 관음전 The Coastal Avalokitesvara Hall	79
해운대 해무 Sea Fog at Haeundae	81
길 A Way	82
목포 비너스 Venus at Mokpo	85
유달산 목포 Mt. Yudal Mokpo	87
유달산 정상 Mt. Yudal Summit	89
남녘 바다 휴양지 South Sea Resort	91
번천의 생각 Beoncheon Thought Thinking of Flipping the Sky	93
끝과 시작 The End and the Beginning	95
문득 심해 Suddenly under the Deep Sea	96
소박 Humbleness	99
순교의 땅 The Land of Martyrdom	101
정적 Still Quietness	102
저 불렀어요? You Called Me?	105

사람과 그 생각
People and the Thoughts

세월의 공존 Coexistence of Ages	109
증인 A Witness	111
입추 불가 No More Room Possible	112
자유로의 길 A Way Toward Freedom	115
가왕 조용필 The King Singer Jo Yong-Pil	117
역사 History	119
열광 Enthusiasm	121
동행 Accompany	123
집중 Concentration	125
석별 A Reluctant Separation	126
국제공항 입국 출구 International Airport Arrival Exit	129
80년 불통 Blocked for Eighty Years	131
탈북 경로 The Routes of Defecting North Korea	133
진심 축하 Heartful Congratulations	135
다산 축복 The Blessing of Fecundity	137

1부

생활의 새 발견
Life's New Discovery

전원주택의 벚꽃

고즈넉한 양평 산촌의 봄날
기와지붕도 토담도 숨결 고른데
철 따라 만개한 벚꽃만 잔칫집이네

Cherry blossoms of a Country House

A Spring day in the quiet calm Yangpyeong mountain village
While the tiled roof and stone walls are in the calm breath
Only the seasonally fully bloomed cherry flowers are partying

눈꽃 1

한적하게 숨죽인 오솔길 산책로
눈꽃 핀 환상의 숲으로 탈바꿈하다
흰 눈이 내려앉은 나목裸木의 풍정風情
가지마다 꽃이 되는 두 번째 봄이다

Snow Flowers 1

The promenade of the trail quietly holding its breath

Transforms into a forest of fantasy where snow flowers bloomed

The scenery of naked trees with snow sitting on

With every branch becoming a flower it is the second Spring

눈꽃 2

소설에서 대설로 가는 계절에
때를 잊고 만개한 백화白花의 얼굴
이 추위 없었으면 못 볼 뻔했네

Snow Flowers 2

In the season moving towards deep winter

The face of a white flower fully bloomed forgetting its time

Almost unable to see were it not for this cold

눈꽃 미소

한 세기를 관통한 작가의 세계
함박눈 덮인 묘소에서 곱게 웃다
생전에도 그랬던 한결같은 품성이다

Snow Flowers' Smile

The writer's world that penetrated through a century
Smiles prettily in the grave covered with thick snowflakes
The nature that never changed even in his lifetime

눈 마당

소나기마을 중앙광장
폭설 첫눈에 맑고 청청하다
밤새 남몰래 옷 갈아입었다

The Snowy Yard

The central plaza of Sonagi Village

Clear and thick blue by the first heavy snow

Changed its clothes in secret over the night

눈을 진 노송

황순원 묘역 산책로 초입
그 정신을 지키는 노송 한 그루
흰 눈 이고지고 여전히 의연하네

An Old Tree with Snow on Its Back

At the Entrance to the promenade to Hwang Sun Won Grave
An old tree keeping the spirit
Unchanged with white snow on its head and back

설경 문학관

가을날 수숫단 같은 원추형 지붕
눈 내린 겨울날에 한껏 고즈넉하네
이 소박한 품위 작가는 짐작 했을까

The Snowy Scenery Literary Museum

The cone roof like an Autumn-day millet sheaf
How calmly cozy in the winter day with heavy snow
Could the writer of humble decency conjecture

애틋한 사랑 마타리꽃

이 꽃말 가진 꽃에 진달래도 있던데
15년을 작은 키로 있던 자리에
올해는 어른 키 높이로 자랄 줄이야
청명한 소나기마을 늦여름 어느 오후

The Earnest Love Yellow Patrinia

Among the flowers with this flower metaphor was azalea too
In the place where it stayed in small height for fifteen years
This year who knew it would grow to an adult's height
One clear blue afternoon in the late summer of Sonagi Village

황금 깃발

쉬는 날 소나기마을의 뜰 고요하다
황엽黃葉의 가을 선언 절정에 이르러
정지된 풍경 속에서도 열변으로 들린다

Golden Flag

On a resting day the Sonagi Village yard is quiet
Yellow leaves announce Autumn reaches its peak
Even in the still scenery its eloquence sounds passionate

북창삼우 北窓三友

초봄 고즈넉한 북향 서재의 창변
세 벗 중 술과 거문고는 없으나
연초록 시심은 흔연히 함께 있네
그대 보다시피 청양 목왕 아닌가

Bukchang Samwoo North Window Three Friends

Early Spring by the window of the study facing North
Although there was no wine or zither among the three friends
There was the joyful light green poetic heart
As thou see isn't it a clear warm Spring

발자국

사람의 마을을 향하여

태초 이래 지속한 인류의 학습

혹여 거기 내 친인의 숨결 있을까

Footprints

Toward a village of people

Ever-lasting mankind's learning since the world started

By any chance will there be any breath of my relatives

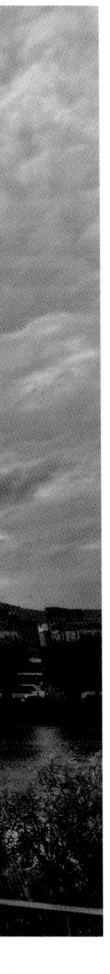

양수리 찬가

두물머리와 세미원이 기다리는 곳
한여름 하늘의 모색 강물에 잠길 때
그대 양수리에서 같이 살 생각 없는가

Praise for Yangsuri Village

Where Dumulmeori and Semiwon are waiting
When the mid-summer sky's setting sun goes under the river
Won't you be interested in living in Yangsuri together

적송

고즈넉한 푸른 산 중동에
밝은 길 몇 가닥
해묵은 소나무 몇 그루
그윽한 눈길로 지켜보고 섰네

Red Pine

In the midway of a quiet calm green mountain
Some bright strands of ways
Some aged pine trees
Stood looking deep in peaceful eyes

휴식

좀 편안하게 내버려 두세요
이 한 철 바쁘게 물살을 갈랐어요
배가 쉬면 사람도 쉬잖아요

Rest

Please let alone for comfort

Busy running through water currents this one season

Don't people also rest if a boat rests

모색 暮色

땅끝마을 바닷길 너머 선착장
고된 일과를 마친 노을이 떴네
천 리길 나그네로 찾아온 눈에
곤비함이 저토록 황홀하다니!

Sunsetting Evening

At the earth-end village wharf beyond the sea way
The twilight rose after a hard day's work
To the eyes of a wanderer from a thousand-ri distance
How is exhaustion that ecstatic

2부

소공녀의 축일
A Little Princess's Festival Days

곰돌이

곁에 호랑이도 있는데
애가 더 만만해요
오래 친했거던요
아무 생각 없이
이렇게 만나러 오곤 해요

Teddy Bear

Although there is a tiger nearby

More comfortable with this bear

Because we have a long friendship

Without any hesitation

We would come like this

궁리

세계 일등 커피 체인이라길래
나 한 번 와 보았지
진열장에 있던 것 무엇이 나을까
생각하고 또 생각하면 답이 있겠지

Much Thinking

Because it is said the world's first-class coffee chain
I came to check once
Which will be better among those on display cabinet
An answer will be there if I think and think

균형

아직은 쉽지 않네
몸의 구심점 찾기가 만만치 않아
좀 오래 걸릴거야
마음의 다림추도 배워야 하거든

A Balance

Not easy yet

Not despisable to find the body's central gravity

It may take a little long time

Need to learn the mind's plumb too

기다리는 마음

누가 일러주지 않아도
문명의 이기利器 앞 지키고 섰네
이 엘리베이터 내 앞에 설 때
우리 엄마 내리지 않을까

Waiting Mind

Although nobody told her

She stood before the facility of the civilization

When this elevator stops in front of me

Won't my mom get out

만보기

다른 동무들 쉬는 시간에도
열심히 운동하는 어린이
이다음에 육상선수 되려나
오늘도 만보를 훨씬 넘겠네

A Ten-thousand Pace Counter

Even at the time other friends take a rest

This child exercises hard

Is she going to be a sprinter

I think it will be far more than ten thousand steps today too

맑음

아직 어린 새싹이지만

될성부른 나무 떡잎부터 다르다고

그 해맑은 얼굴에 장밋빛 내일 있네

Clearness

Although it's still a young new sprout

The seed leaf of a promising tree is different

There's a rosy tomorrow on that pure clear face

모닝 빵순이

어느결에 서양식 입맛을 익혀
일용할 양식의 메뉴를 바꿨네
풍성한 단품 식탁의 축복!
예로부터 밥이 하늘이라 했느니

Morning Bread Girl

When did she acquire the Western style appetite
Daily food menus changed
The blessing by the table of rich single food
From time old meals are said to be the sky

소공녀

메리 고 어라운드 목마를 타고
어젯밤 꿈꾸던 세상을 생각한다
귀하고 소중한 것 모두 여기 있다

A Little Princess

Riding the wooden horse of a merry go around
Thinking of the world dreamed of last night
Everything rare and valuable is here

아침 운동

튼튼한 몸에 튼튼한 마음
성공은 노력하는 자의 편
등에 업은 아이에게도 배운다는데
지나고 보니 헛되이 보낸 세월이 많네

Morning Exercise

A strong mind in a strong body
Success is on the side of those making efforts
As said we learn even from the child on our backs
Time passed and I found I sent a lot of ages in vain

어린 예술가

그 속에 타고난 숨은 기질이 있는지
진지하고 집중적이며 감각이 있네
고흐도 피카소도 시작은 미약했을 터

A Child Artist

Is there a hidden nature born inside
She has a sincere focusing sense
Gogh and Picasso's beginnings might also have been weak

위니비니 천국

소공녀 생일날보다 더 화려해
젤리볼 캔디팩 고르기 어렵네
구멍가게보다 외려 사기 힘들어
걍 아이쇼핑으로 지나가 보려네

Weeny Beeny Heaven

More splendid than the little princess's birthday
Jelly balls and candy packs difficult to choose
Rather harder to buy than in a small store
Well I may try passing through only with eye shopping

작은 공주님

동화 나라 나들이 온 어린 공주님
한 손에는 영예 또 한 손에는 온정
이 모습 오래도록 기념비처럼 남으리

Dear Little Princess

A child princess came to a fairy world on a picnic
An honor on one hand and a warm affection on the other
May this appearance remain long like a monument

전문가

손질해서 판매하는 어려운 일을
복장과 장비 갖추고 시작하려나
어린 요리사의 풋풋한 결심을 보네

An Expert

The difficult work of selling after preparing by hand
Is she going to start she got the outfit and equipment
Can see a child cook's sweet resolution

조손 합심

고사리 손으로 김밥 말기
세상만사 마음에 달렸나니
이 초심이면 명 쉐프 되겠네

Grandmother and Granddaughter's Cooperation

Rolling gimbab with little hands
Isn't everything depending on the mind
With this original mind can be a renowned chef

청명

맑고 밝고 편안한 웃음
이 얼굴로 내일 향해 나가면
날마다 때마다 이르는 곳마다
세상이 온통 환하겠네

Bright Clearness

Clear bright comfortable smile
With this face if she goes toward her tomorrow
Everyday every time wherever she reaches
The world will be all bright

3부

풍경 속의 잔상
Unforgettable Images of Scenery

양양 휴휴암 앞바다

산과 바다가 어우러진 곳
해안 절벽 아래 저 넓은 암반
모두가 세월의 풍화를 이겼네

The Sea off Hyu-hyu Rock Yangyang

Where the mountains and the sea go together
The wide rock table under the coastal cliff
All beat the erosion by ages

해변 관음전

왜 바닷가에 지었을까
중생의 고뇌를 씻어주고
환난을 구제하는 그 원력願力이
바다처럼 광활하기 때문일까

The Coastal Avalokitesvara Hall

Why built by the sea
Washing off people's suffering
Saving from afflictions that prime power
Like the sea is expansive maybe that's why

해운대 해무

마천루 중동을 휘감아 도는 안개
몇 사람이 줄지어 바라보고 섰네
여름 해변 모랫벌의 결고운 뒷그림
내 삶 어딘가에 숨은 쉼표 한 장면

Sea Fog at Haeundae

The fog winding around the skyscrapers

Some people stand in line looking up

The background painting of fine summer beach sand field

A scene of a comma hidden somewhere in my life

길

하늘길 뱃길이 사뭇 서로 다른 줄
눈으로 보고서야 밝히 알겠네
아하! 거기 인생사 비의秘義 한 자락

A Way

The sky way and the sea way are quite different from each other
Not until seeing with eyes was it clear
Aha! There the one hem of subtle meaning of human history

목포 비너스

유달산 해상 케이블카의 선물
창으로 비친 아리따운 여성상
그 산의 정령처럼 아래를 굽어보네

Venus at Mokpo

The gift of the Mt. Yudal maritime cable car
A pretty woman image reflected on the window
Looks down with her head bent like the mountain spirit

유달산 목포

노적봉 아래 먼 도시, 님 자취 간곳없다
애달픈 정조, 예나 지금이나 매한가진데
목포의 눈물 닮아 하늘조차 흐렸다

Mt. Yudal Mokpo

The city far under Nojok Peak, the trace of my love is nowhere

The heartbreaking sentiments, in the past or now all the same kind

Taking after Mokpo's tears even the sky is overcast

유달산 정상

누가 이렇게 공들여 쌓았을까
여러 얼굴 층층이 정상을 이루었네
호남의 금강산 그 고운 별호도 얻고

Mt. Yudal Summit

Who endeavored to stack up like this
Several faces on top of another achieved the summit
Mt Kumgang of Honam that charming nickname it got

남녘 바다 휴양지

목포 아래 남단 진도 바닷가
유럽풍 외관으로 새로 지은 쉼터
몸이 쉴 때 비로소 마음도 쉬느니

South Sea Resort

Jindo Seaside down south Mokpo
A newly built resting place in European style appearance
When the body rests so does the mind

번천翻天의 생각

달에서 방아 찧던 토끼는 간곳없고
지상의 토끼 가족 가운데 달을 두었네
리조트 마당에 펼쳐둔 부드러운 상상력

Beoncheon Thought Thinking of Flipping the Sky

The rabbits pounding the pestles in the moon are nowhere
Among the family of the rabbits on this planet is the moon left
On the resort yard spread the soft imagination

끝과 시작

전남 해남의 땅끝에 서서
우리 삶의 시작과 끝을 생각하네
이 도돌이표의 종점은 어디일까
공空과 색色이 하나라는데

The End and the Beginning

Standing on the earth end of Haenam Jeonnam
I am thinking of the beginning and the end of our lives
Where will this repeat mark end
Changeability and physical status are said to be the one

문득 심해

스쿠버 다이빙 하지 않아도
황홀한 해저 바닥에 이르네
세계 제일 인천공항
언제부터 이렇게 당연했던가

Suddenly under the Deep Sea

Even without scuba diving

The amazing sea bottom reached

The world first class Incheon International airport

Since when has it been taken for granted like this

소박 素朴

축소지향의 나라 일본
참 고요한 어린이 독서방
손님 기다리는 탁상이 둘
그런데도 내내 비인간非人間일세

Humbleness

Japan the nation preferring smallness
Children's truly quiet reading room
The tables waiting for guests are two
Despite so non-human all the time

순교의 땅

일본 초기 카톨릭의 성녀
호소카와 가라샤가 숨진 자리
기념비는 사뭇 의연한데
빌 데가 여러 모양으로 늘었네

The Land of Martyrdom

The holy woman of the early Catholic Japan
The place where Hosokawa Garasha breathed the last
The memorial stone is quite unchanged
Places for offering a prayer has increased in several ways

정적

다마츠쿠리성당의 본당
일본 가톨릭 성인 26위 그림이
뒷벽에서 굽어보는 고요한 정경
예수 달린 십자가 황금으로 빛나네
저절로 거룩하고 경건한 공간

Still Quietness

The main hall of Damatskuri Catholic Church
The twenty-six holy Japanese Catholic saints' pictures
Looking down from the back walls in the quiet scene
The cross Jesus hanging on shines bright in gold
The space getting holy and devout on its own

저 불렀어요?

신오사카역 행인 가운데
뉘 부르는 소리 들린 듯하여
돌아보니 일행 모두 앞서갔네
시공을 넘어선 환각의 음성일까

You Called Me?

New Osaka Station among the company
Because it seemed I heard somebody calling me out
Looked back to find all the company went ahead
Was that a voice of hallucination beyond time and space

4부

사람과 그 생각
People and the Thoughts

세월의 공존

가황 나훈아의 고별 무대다
28년 전 자신과 함께 부르는 노래
같은 사람이면서 같지 않은 사람
여기 남모르는 이야기가 숨어 있다

Coexistence of Ages

The farewell stage by the emperor singer Na Huna
The songs he sang together with himself of twenty-eight years ago
While he is the same person he is not
Here the stories others don't know stay hidden

증인

왜 역대 대통령 11명 사진을 걸었을까
그 장구한 기간의 역사를 지켜보았네
그의 시국관조차 가슴 울리는 이유일세

A Witness

Why hang the successive eleven presidents' pictures
Kept looking at the history of that long period
That's why even his political stance rings my heart

입추立錐 불가

고마웠습니다!
58년 가황歌皇의 별빛으로 살았기에
이 넓은 공연장에 발 디딜 틈 없다

No More Room Possible

Been grateful for you!
Lived as the light of an emperor singer star
This wide performance arena has no room for more feet

자유로의 길

거장은 죽지 않는다
다만 사라져갈 뿐이다
그대 새 인생 행로의 개막에
존경을 다하여 기립 갈채한다

A Way Toward Freedom

The maestro does not die
Only to go disappearing
To thee on the opening of a new path of life
From the full respect give a standing ovation

가왕歌王 조용필

왜 뒷모습일까
머지않아 내려온다는 신호
반백 년 세월을 함께한 여정
무대 떠나도 노래는 남을 터

The King Singer Jo Yong-Pil

Why his back is in view
A signal he may step down before long
A journey together for half a century
The stage leaves but the songs will remain

역사

한국 대중 가요사의 한 페이지
장르를 넘나들며 20집 앨범
음악에도 작은 거인이 있다네

History

A page of Korean popular song history
Crossing the genres his 20th album
Even in music there is a little giant

열광

그가 있어 탄생한 오빠 부대
이 운집과 환호, 그를 위한 것일까?
아닐세!
내 마음속 불꽃이 찾은, 내 삶의 값

Enthusiasm

He being there was the Oppa fan unit born
This gathering and joyful shouts, are for him?
No!
The flame in my heart found, the value of my life

동행

사막 샹그릴라를 노래하는 정태춘
노래를 시라 말하는 또 한 사람
예전에 김광석이 그러더니
시인이 가수 되기는 쉬워도
그 역방향의 동행은 어려운 일인데

Accompany

Jeong Tae Chun singing Desert Shangri-La
Here one more person saying a song is a poem
Kim Kwang Seok said so too
Easy as it is for a poet to become a singer
Accompanying in a reverse direction is a hard matter

집중

정태춘 박은옥 부부 콘서트
문득 떠오른 정호승 시 한 편
'맹인 부부 가수!'
참 소박하고 순수한 무대이기에

Concentration

The concert by the couple Jeong Tae Chun and Park Eun Ok
Suddenly reminds me of a poem by Jeong Ho Sung
'Blind Couple Singers!'
As it is a truly humble and pure stage

석별

애기 때부터 네 해를 함께 산 우리 토리
환경이 달라져 눈물로 너를 보내느니
부디 야속한 우리를 잊고 잘 살아다오

A Reluctant Separation

From its baby time for four years our Tori lived with us
For the environment change we send you away in tears
Make sure you forget this heartless us and live well

국제공항 입국 출구

저마다의 생각 담은 뒷모습으로
그 애틋한 이를 기다리나니
이 순간만큼 행복한 출영出迎이 있을까

International Airport Arrival Exit

With the back views containing each one's thinking
Waiting for the lovely ones
Will there be a reception as happy as this moment

느린우체통

언젠가 통일 한반도에

살고 있을

80년 불통

서울 강서구 남북통합문화센터 한 구석
북한 고향으로 보내는 편지 우체통 있네
오죽하면 느리게 간다고 써 두었을까
분단 80년이 넘도록 아직도 막혀있는 길

Blocked for Eighty Years

One corner of Inter-Korea Uni-Cultural Center Kangseo Seoul
A postbox is there for the letters going to hometowns in North Korea
How slow it was a writing's left down there
Until over 80 years of separation has the road been still blocked

탈북 경로

남북통합문화센터 소전시실
젊은 조형 작가의 눈물 어린 고백
신발 바닥에 적힌 북한 중국 한국 경로마다
애절한 심경으로 부모님께 드린 현장 소식

The Routes of Defecting North Korea

A small exhibition room in Inter-Korea Uni-Cultural Center
Tearful confession by a young formative artist
Every route in North Korea China and Korea put on the soles
From his pathetic heart to his parents reported the on-spot happenings

오늘을 걷는 이유 2025

생사를 알 길 없는 두고 온 가족에 대한 그리움과 죄책감은 가슴 시리게 아프지만
때론 가족의 몫까지 살아내야 되는 이유이며,
삐걱거리는 톱니바퀴에 윤활유와도 같이 계속해 걸어갈 수 있는 원동력이 되기도 한다.
어떤 형태로든 가족에 대한 그리움과 추억은 나에겐 큰 힘이 된다.

"오늘의 걸음이 있기까지 하루하루의 원동력이 되어주는
나의 가족... 고맙습니다."

진심 축하

여행지에서 벗들이 차린
소박한 생일상
사정 급할 땐 가장 경제적으로!
마음부터 모으니 그저 진수성찬

Heartful Congratulations

Friends prepared in a travel destination
A humble birthday table
When desperate be the most economical!
As hearts first collected it's just a sumptuous feast

다산 축복

못 미침이 지나침보다 낫다는데
이 풍성한 결실은 옛말이 무색하네
단단하고 작은 꽃사과 먹을 날 올까
익어가는 모양 보기에도 아까운데

The Blessing of Fecundity

Falling short is said to be better than going too far
This rich fruit put the old saying ashamed
Will there be a day of eating the hard little crab apples
Can't waste the way they are ripening even by looking at it

김종회 디카시집

북창삼우
Bukchang Samwoo

지은이 김종회 **초판인쇄** 2025년 11월 10일 **초판발행** 2025년 11월 15일 **펴낸곳** 도서출판 상상인 **편집주간** 황정산 **펴낸이** 진혜진 **기획·마케팅** 전은빈 최유림 노혜림 정현수 **책임교정** 오 늘 **편집** 세종PNP **등록번호** 제572-96-00959호 **등록일자** 2019년 6월 25일 **주소** 06621 서울시 서초구 서초대로74길 29, 904호 **전화번호** 02-747-1367, 010-7371-1871 **팩스** 02-747-1877 **전자우편** ssaangin@hanmail.net

ISBN 979-11-7490-025-8 (03810)

값 14,000원

* 이 책은 전부 또는 일부 내용을 재사용하려면 반드시 저작권자와 도서출판 상상인의 동의를 받아야 합니다
* 이 도서의 국립중앙도서관 출판시도서목록(CIP)은 서지정보유통지원시스템 홈페이지(http://seoji.nl.go.kr)와 국가자료공동목록시스템(http://www.nl.go.kr/kolisnet)에서 이용하실 수 있습니다.